Indian Cooking

Learn Authentic Indian Cooking with
Easy Indian Recipes

By
BookSumo Press
All rights reserved

Published by
http://www.booksumo.com

Table of Contents

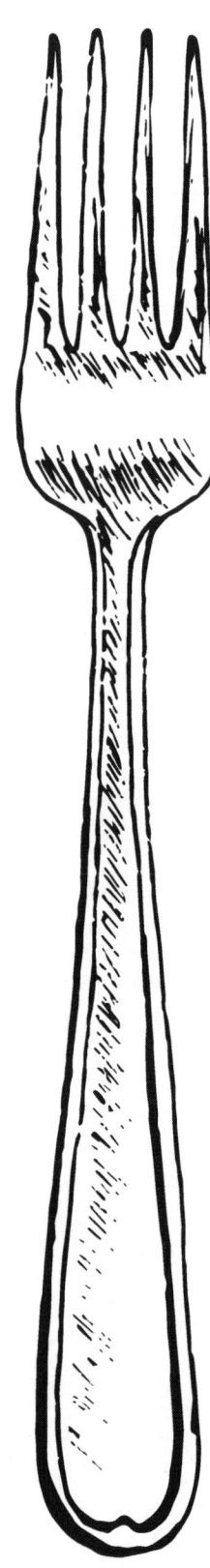

Spicy Mango Chicken 7

Grilled Tandoori II 8

Tomato Chicken Indian Style 10

Korma 12

Spinach Dahl 14

Masoor Daal 15

Indian Style Eggplant 16

Aloo Gobi 18

Curry Shrimp 19

Curry Fish 20

Chicken Biryani 22

Brown Rice, Chicken, Curry, Casserole 24

Aloo Matar 25

Potatoes Indian Style 26

Dahl II 27

Okra Curry 28

Lentil, Tomato Soup, Indian Style 29

Indian Style Salsa 30

Vegan Classical Indian Style Relish 31

Northern Indian Chickpeas 32

Sabji 33

Tacos Indian Style 34

Tandoori Pizza 35

South Indian Style Crepes 36

Lassi 37

Kolkata Style Pudding 38

A Fruity Salad in Indian 39

Authentic Saag 40

Spicy Masala Cauliflower 41

Homemade Makhani 42

Kebabs From Mumbai 43

Ginger Coconut Curry Chicken 44

An Indian Breakfast Cereal 45

Standard Oven Roasted Samosas 46

Curry Russets Indian Style 47

Chai for Chatting 48

Basmaati Rice 101 49

Spicy Beef Roast Hyderabadi Inspired 50

Kerala Curry 52

Southern Coconut Curry 53

Priyanka's Butter Chicken 54

Anglo-Indian Curry 55

Curried Chicken Breasts 56

Manhattan Restaurant Indian Curry 57

Caribbean Coconut Curry 58

North Indian Inspired Curry 59

How to Make Tikka Masala 60

Inner City Curry 61

Pineapple Pepper Curry 62

Cape Chicken Curry 63

Anjali's Carrot and Zucchini Curry 64

Backyard Tandoori 65

Classical Korma 66

Emerald Isle Curry 67

Tuesday's Curry 68

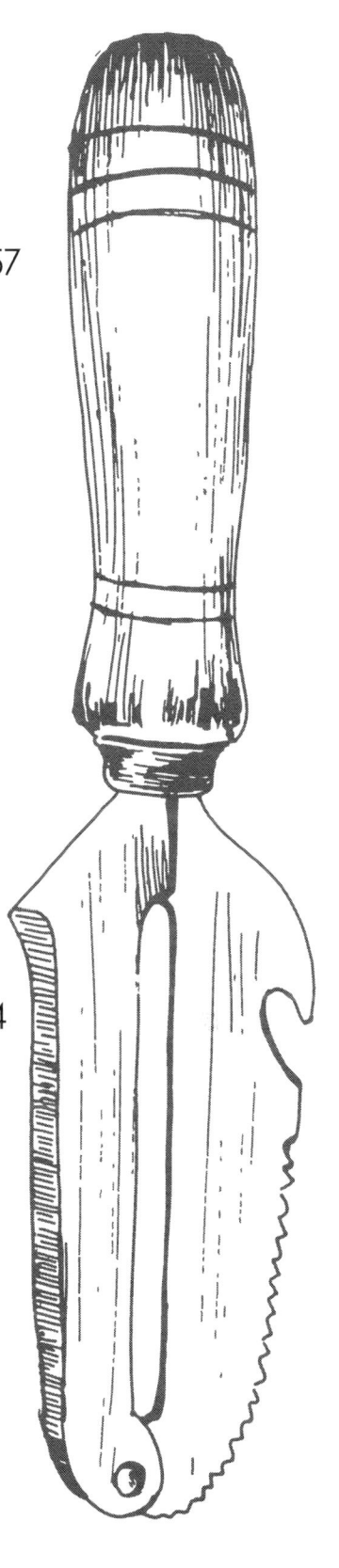

Chicken Curry 101 69

Curry Dump Dinner 70

Simple Fruit Curry 71

Spicy Mango Chicken

🥣 Prep Time: 25 mins
⏲ Total Time: 35 mins

Servings per Recipe: 4
Calories   398 kcal
Carbohydrates   31.1 g
Cholesterol   58 mg
Fat   20.4 g
Protein   26.5 g
Sodium   179 mg

Ingredients

- 2 medium mangoes, peeled and sliced, divided
- One (10 ounce) can coconut milk
- 4 tsps vegetable oil
- 4 tsps spicy curry paste
- 14 ounces skinless, boneless chicken breast halves - cut into cubes
- 4 medium shallots, sliced
- One large English cucumber, seeded and sliced

Directions

1. Grab your blender and get it ready for some work.
2. Combine mango slices and coconut milk in the blender and blend it up until paste like. Place these contents aside.
3. Get a cooking pot and put some oil in it and heat everything with a medium level of heat. Once the oil is hot add your curry paste and let everything fry until you can smell a great aroma. This should take about one min.
4. Get the shallots and the chicken. Add these things to the curry oil and fry it all down until the chicken is fully cooked and your shallots are nice and soft. This should take about five mins of frying.
5. Grab your mango mixture from the blender and fry it down as well with the chicken and shallots.
6. Before serving add some more mango pieces and also some cucumbers.
7. Let cool. Enjoy.

GRILLED
Tandoori II

Prep Time: 10 mins
Total Time: 8 hrs 55 mins

Servings per Recipe: 8
Calories	349 kcal
Carbohydrates	5.4 g
Cholesterol	120 mg
Fat	20.5 g
Protein	34.2 g
Sodium	618 mg

Ingredients

2 (6 ounce) containers plain yogurt
2 tsps kosher salt
One tsp black pepper
1/2 tsp ground cloves
2 tbsps freshly grated ginger
3 cloves garlic, minced
4 tsps paprika
2 tsps ground cumin
2 tsps ground cinnamon
2 tsps ground coriander
16 chicken thighs
olive oil spray

Directions

1. Get yourself a medium sized container for mixing the following ingredients: ginger, yoghurt, cloves, salt, pepper, and salt (a bowl would be ideal).
2. Also combine the following taking care to mix all the contents together evenly: coriander, garlic, cinnamon, paprika, and cumin.
3. Set this mixture to the side to settle and move on to the next step.
4. Grab your chicken and clean it under some water (ideally cold water).
5. After the chicken has been cleaned. Dry it with napkins or paper towels (apply a patting motion for best drying results).
6. Now you want to take your chicken and mix it with the yogurt mixture we made earlier. In a large plastic bag that is reseal-able. Make sure that after you have added the chicken and yogurt to the bag you remove all the air which will be trapped inside.
7. Work the bag by turning it upside down and shaking it lightly to evenly dispense mixture and cover all the chicken.
8. Put this bag of chicken in a container and place it in the frig for at least 8 hours (ideally you would allow this to marinate overnight) reposition the bag occasionally (not necessary but recommended).
9. Get your grill ready. Set it to a medium level of heat and cover the grate with oil or a non

stick cooking spray.
10. Remove each piece of chicken from the bag and spray it with olive oil. Place it on the grill.
11. Allow each piece of chicken to receive direct heat for 2 minutes.
12. Then turn each piece of chicken and allow for direct heat for another 2 mins.
13. Move each piece of chicken to the side of the grill and let it receive indirect heat for at least 25 to 35 mins and make sure the internal temperature of the meat is at least 180 degrees Fahrenheit.
14. Remove from grill, plate, and serve.
15. Throw away the remaining seasoning left over in the bag.

TOMATO
Chicken Indian Style

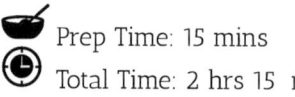

Prep Time: 15 mins
Total Time: 2 hrs 15 mins

Servings per Recipe: 6
Calories   134 kcal
Carbohydrates   6.9 g
Cholesterol   57 mg
Fat   5.4 g
Protein   14.7 g
Sodium   547 mg

Ingredients

One large onion, chopped
4 cloves garlic, chopped
One slice fresh ginger root
One tbsp olive oil
2 tsps ground cumin
One tsp ground turmeric
One tsp salt
One tsp ground black pepper
1/2 tsp ground cardamom
One (One inch) piece cinnamon stick
1/4 tsp ground cloves

2 bay leaves
1/4 tsp ground nutmeg
6 skinless chicken thighs
One (14.5 ounce) can whole peeled tomatoes, crushed

Directions

1. Plug in your food processor and place some ginger, onion, and garlic into it.
2. Turn the processor on and process these ingredients into a smooth mixture.
3. Next grab a frying pan or skillet, and add some oil to it. Heat the pan and the oil with a medium level of heat.
4. Once the pan and oil is heated grab your paste and combine it with the oil. Make sure to constantly stir the paste and oil to avoid burning.
5. Let the contents cook for 10 mins.
6. Add to your paste the following ingredients: nutmeg, cumin, bay leaves, salt, cloves, pepper, cinnamon, and cardamom.
7. Combine and mix all the above ingredients making sure to stir consistently for about 2 minutes until you smell a good aroma of spice and seasoning.
8. Now grab your chicken pieces and combine them with the paste making sure they are evenly covered with the seasoning.

9. Combine and cook the new mixture for about 4 mins making sure you are continually stirring.
10. After 4 mins. Add tomatoes.
11. Lower the temperature of the heat to low and let everything nicely simmer for a few hours (ideally 2 hrs).
12. When you notice a splitting of the oil from the mixture begin to stir. Make sure you have the pan covered lest you will have to add water every once and a while.

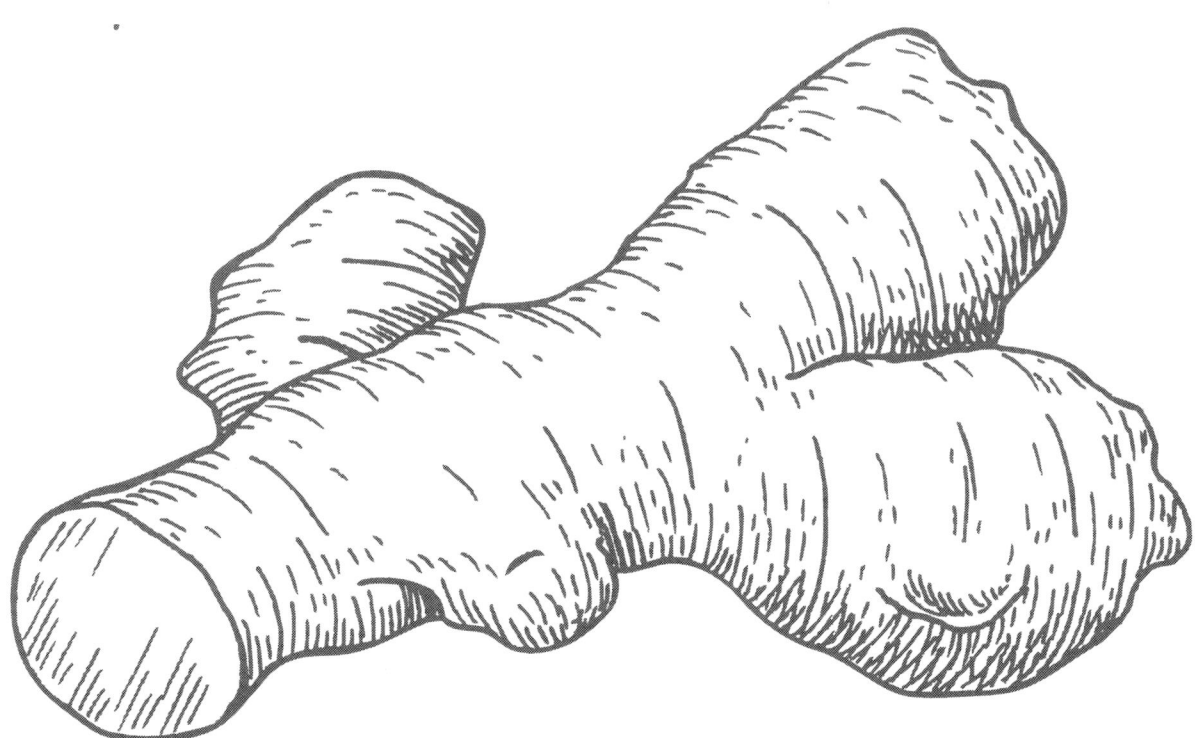

KORMA

Prep Time: 20 mins
Total Time: 1 hr

Servings per Recipe: 4
Calories 398 kcal
Carbohydrates 13.4 g
Cholesterol 95 mg
Fat 27.5 g
Protein 25.3 g
Sodium 477 mg

Ingredients

1/4 cup cashew halves
1/4 cup boiling water
3 cloves garlic, peeled
One (1/2 inch) piece fresh ginger root, peeled and chopped
3 tbsps vegetable oil
2 bay leaves, crumbled
One large onion, minced
One tsp ground coriander
One tsp garam masala
One tsp ground cumin
One tsp ground turmeric
One tsp chili powder
3 skinless, boneless chicken breast halves - diced
1/4 cup tomato sauce
One cup chicken broth
1/2 cup heavy cream
1/2 cup plain yogurt
One tsp cornstarch, mixed with equal parts water

Directions

1. Grab a small container and combine the boiling water with cashews. Allow this mixture to sit for about 20 mins.
2. Get your food processor ready for work. Add garlic and ginger inside the processor and work the contents until they become a paste. Once the contents are a paste set it to the side.
3. Grab a skillet or wok and add some oil and get it nice and hot with some medium heat.
4. Add your bay leaves to the oil and let it cook. Bay leaves should fry for about half of a minute.
5. Now you should add some onion to the oil and fry them down until translucent (three to five mins).
6. Get your food processor contents (ginger and garlic) and combine it with the onions and let everything fry for five minutes.

7. Combine with the mixture the following seasonings: chili powder, coriander, turmeric, masala, and cumin.
8. Combine your chicken with the seasoning and fry it for five minutes. Now combine your chicken broth as well as your tomato sauce. Make sure that you cover this pot, and lower the temperature.
9. Let everything slowly simmer for 15 mins. Make sure to stir the contents every once and a while.
10. Grab that food processor again and throw in some cashews and their accompanying water into the food processor with some yogurt and cream. Mix it all together until paste like.
11. Now take your food processor mixture and combine it with the chicken let everything cook for another 15 mins.
12. Finally combine the cornstarch and let everything go for an additional 2 mins.
13. Let food cool.
14. Plate it. Serve it. Enjoy it.

SPINACH
Dahl

Prep Time: 10 mins
Total Time: 40 mins

Servings per Recipe: 4
Calories   362 kcal
Carbohydrates   44.9 g
Cholesterol   15 mg
Fat   13.4 g
Protein   21 g
Sodium   693 mg

Ingredients

One 1/2 cups red lentils
3 1/2 cups water
1/2 tsp salt
1/2 tsp ground turmeric
1/2 tsp chili powder
One pound spinach, rinsed and chopped
2 tbsps butter

One onion, chopped
One tsp ground cumin
One tsp mustard seed
One tsp garam masala
1/2 cup coconut milk

Directions

1. First step is to take your lentils and put them in a container filled with water for about 20 minutes (soak everything).
2. Grab a large pan, add some water, and boil it. Once the water is boiling combine the following ingredients: chili powder, salt, turmeric, and lentils.
3. Now you need to cover the pot and get it boiling again. Once you have the pot boiling immediately turn the temperature down to get a nice simmer going.
4. You want everything to simmer for approx. 15 mins. Now add your spinach to the simmering goodness and let it simmer and cook for another five mins. At this point you should notice your lentils are nice and soft (if not continue simmering). Remember to add more water if you think it is needed.
5. Grab another pan. This time a smaller one.
6. Place the new pan over medium heat and combine the following ingredients: mustard seeds, melted butter, cumin, and onion. Make sure that you are stirring this mixture constantly. Cook everything down until the onions are transparent. Once you find that your onions are transparent combine the mixture with the lentils from earlier.
7. Finally combine lentils with coconut milk, and garam masala.
8. Heat everything for a few more mins (2 mins). Let contents cool. Plate and enjoy.

Masoor Daal

🥣 Prep Time: 5 mins
🕐 Total Time: 35 mins

Servings per Recipe: 4
Calories   185 kcal
Carbohydrates   25 g
Cholesterol   0 mg
Fat   5.2 g
Protein   11.1 g
Sodium   868 mg

Ingredients

One cup red lentils
One slice ginger, One inch piece, peeled
1/4 tsp ground turmeric
One tsp salt
1/2 tsp cayenne pepper, or to taste

4 tsps vegetable oil
4 tsps dried minced onion
One tsp cumin seeds

Directions

1. First step when dealing with lentils is to clean them. So run the lentils through water until the water runs clear.
2. Grab a sauce pan and place your clean lentils in it with the following seasonings: cayenne pepper, ginger, salt, and turmeric.
3. Take all these ingredients and submerge them in water inside of your sauce pan. Get everything to nicely boil. Make sure that you remove any foam which manifests during the boiling process.
4. Lower the temperature and let the contents simmer. Make sure you stir everything every once and a while.
5. Let the food simmer until the lentils are nice and soft and everything looks like a soup.
6. Grab a container that can be put in the microwave. Inside of the container place the following things: cumin seeds, oil, and dried onion.
7. Set the container in the microwave on the highest setting for 45 secs.
8. Get the onions to a brown like color but make sure to not burn them.
9. Take out the microwave contents and combine it with the lentils.
10. Plate, serve, enjoy.

INDIAN STYLE
Eggplant

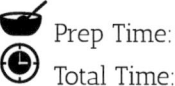
Prep Time: 15 mins
Total Time: 1 hr 5 mins

Servings per Recipe: 4
Calories   119 kcal
Carbohydrates   13.4 g
Cholesterol   0 mg
Fat   7.4 g
Protein   2.4 g
Sodium   300 mg

Ingredients

One eggplant
2 tbsps vegetable oil
1/2 tsp cumin seeds
One medium onion, sliced
One tsp chopped fresh ginger
One large tomato - peeled, seeded and diced
One clove garlic, minced
1/2 tsp ground turmeric
1/2 tsp ground cumin

1/2 tsp ground coriander
1/4 tsp cayenne pepper
1/2 tsp salt, or to taste
ground black pepper to taste
1/4 cup chopped fresh cilantro

Directions

1. For this recipe we will need the broiler. So turn on the broiler and get it hot before continuing.
2. Grab your eggplant and coat it with oil. You can also coat it with cooking spray.
3. Put the eggplant beneath the broiler and let it broil until it becomes soft and you notice the skin peeling off. This will take about 30 minutes. Make sure that you evenly cook the eggplant by turning it.
4. Grab a knife and halve the eggplant from top to bottom.
5. Remove the flesh from the vegetable. Throw away the skin.
6. Once the flesh of the eggplant has been removed dice it up and put it to the side.
7. Grab a frying pan or skillet and put oil in it. Get the pan and oil hot with a medium level of heat.
8. Once the oil is hot add some cumin seeds and let them fry for a bit. You should notice them turn brown but make sure that you do not burn them. While oil is still hot add the following: garlic, onion, and ginger.

9. Make sure that you stir and cook everything until tender.
10. Next combine with the onions your tomatoes and the following other seasonings: black pepper, turmeric, salt, cumin, cayenne and coriander.
11. Let these cook while stirring for a few minutes (2 mins)
12. Now we are ready for the eggplant.
13. Combine your eggplant dices with the frying spices and let it fry until you notice a good amount of the moisture has been removed. This should take about 15 mins.
14. Taste the eggplant and add more seasonings if you so desire.
15. Let the contents cool.
16. Plate and serve. Enjoy.

ALOO Gobi

Prep Time: 10 mins
Total Time: 1 hr 30 mins

Servings per Recipe: 4
Calories   622 kcal
Carbohydrates   64 g
Cholesterol   0 mg
Fat   39.2 g
Protein   13.1 g
Sodium   2172 mg

Ingredients

1/4 cup olive oil
One medium onion, chopped
One tbsp minced garlic
One tsp cumin seeds
One (15 ounce) can diced tomatoes
One (15 ounce) can coconut milk
2 tbsps ground coriander
One tbsp salt
One tbsp ground turmeric
One tbsp cayenne pepper
One tsp ground cinnamon
One tsp ground ginger
One tsp ground cardamom
3 large Yukon Gold potatoes, peeled and cubed
One medium head cauliflower, chopped into bite size pieces
One (15 ounce) can garbanzo beans, drained
2 tbsps garam masala

Directions

1. Get a nice sized pot and place it over a medium heat level with oil and onions. Fry the onions until they are translucent. This typically will take about four mins.
2. Once your onions are translucent then combine some cumin and garlic and continue frying the ingredients until you find your onions are turning a brownish color.
3. Now begin to mix in the following: cardamom, tomatoes, ginger, coconut, cinnamon, coriander, cayenne, salt, and turmeric.
4. Continue to cook the contents until they begin to boil. Once everything is boiling add the garbanzo beans, potatoes, and cauliflower. Take care to mix everything well.
5. Now it is important to lower the cooking temperature to low and place a lid on the cooking pan.
6. Allow everything to simmer nicely until you notice the potatoes are soft. This will take about 45 mins to an hour.
7. Once the potatoes are soft add some garam masala and stir. Let the mixture cook for an additional five mins before serving. Enjoy

Curry Shrimp

Prep Time: 15 mins
Total Time: 30 mins

Servings per Recipe: 4
Calories   416 kcal
Carbohydrates   10.9 g
Cholesterol   146 mg
Fat   32.1 g
Protein   23 g
Sodium   930 mg

Ingredients

- 2 tbsps peanut oil
- 1/2 sweet onion, minced
- 2 cloves garlic, chopped
- One tsp ground ginger
- One tsp ground cumin
- One 1/2 tsps ground turmeric
- One tsp paprika
- 1/2 tsp chili powder
- One (14.5 ounce) can chopped tomatoes
- One (14 ounce) can coconut milk
- One tsp salt
- One pound cooked and peeled shrimp
- 2 tbsps chopped fresh cilantro

Directions

1. Grab a large frying pan or skillet. Place the pan over a medium heating level.
2. As always, add some oil, and some onions.
3. Let these onions cook until you find that they are translucent. This will occur in about four mins.
4. Once the onions are ready take the skillet from the stove and place it to the side for about two mins.
5. Now add the following ingredients to the onions: chili powder, garlic, paprika, ginger, turmeric, and cumin.
6. Place the pan back over a low heating level. Making sure that you are continuously stirring everything.
7. With the pan over a low heat. Add coconut milk and tomatoes and salt to the seasoning. Let everything begin to simmer nicely. Make sure that you stir the contents every once and a while. This simmer process should last for about ten mins.
8. Now add shrimp, with dried and fresh cilantro, to your simmering mixture and let it continue to simmer for another minute or so.
9. At this point the food is ready for serving.
10. Enjoy.

CURRY
Fish

Prep Time: 20 mins
Total Time: 1 hr 25 mins

Servings per Recipe: 4
Calories	338 kcal
Carbohydrates	11.6 g
Cholesterol	56 mg
Fat	13.5 g
Protein	41.6 g
Sodium	2715 mg

Ingredients

2 tsps Dijon mustard
One tsp ground black pepper
1/2 tsp salt
2 tbsps canola oil
4 white fish fillets
One onion, coarsely chopped
4 cloves garlic, roughly chopped
One (One inch) piece fresh ginger root, peeled and chopped
5 cashew halves
One tbsp canola oil

2 tsps cayenne pepper, or to taste
1/2 tsp ground turmeric
One tsp ground cumin
One tsp ground coriander
One tsp salt
One tsp white sugar
1/2 cup chopped tomato
1/4 cup vegetable broth
1/4 cup chopped fresh cilantro

Directions

1. Get a non deep dish for mixing. Combine the following in this dish: 2 tbsps of canola oil, mustard, half a tsp of salt, and some pepper to taste.
2. Now grab the fish pieces and place them into the mixture and make sure to evenly coat them. Place the fish in the frig for at least 30 mins.
3. Now grab a food processor and get it ready for some work.
4. Place the following items into the food processor: cashews, onion, ginger, garlic.
5. Process everything into a nice smooth paste.
6. Place this paste aside for a moment.
7. Now let's get the oven ready.
8. Turn the oven on to 350 degrees Fahrenheit or 175 degrees Celsius for preheating.
9. Now grab a nice frying pan or skillet and heat it up with a medium heating level with one tsp of canola oil.
10. Grab that paste we made earlier and mix it with the hot oil. Make sure to cook and stir the

paste and oil for about two mins.
11. Now combine the following ingredients into the paste for seasoning: sugar, cayenne pepper, one tsp of salt, turmeric, coriander, and cumin.
12. Allow these seasoning to fry for about 5 mins making sure to stir as well.
13. Now grab your veggie broth and diced tomatoes and mix them into the seasonings.
14. Take out your fish and place them on a dish for the oven.
15. Throw away any left-over marinade.
16. Use our seasoning in the pot to coat the fish and let everything cook in the oven for about 30 mins.
17. To determine if your fish is ready grab and fork and see if the fish easily flakes. If so you are ready to garnish it with some cilantro.
18. Plate for serving.
19. Enjoy

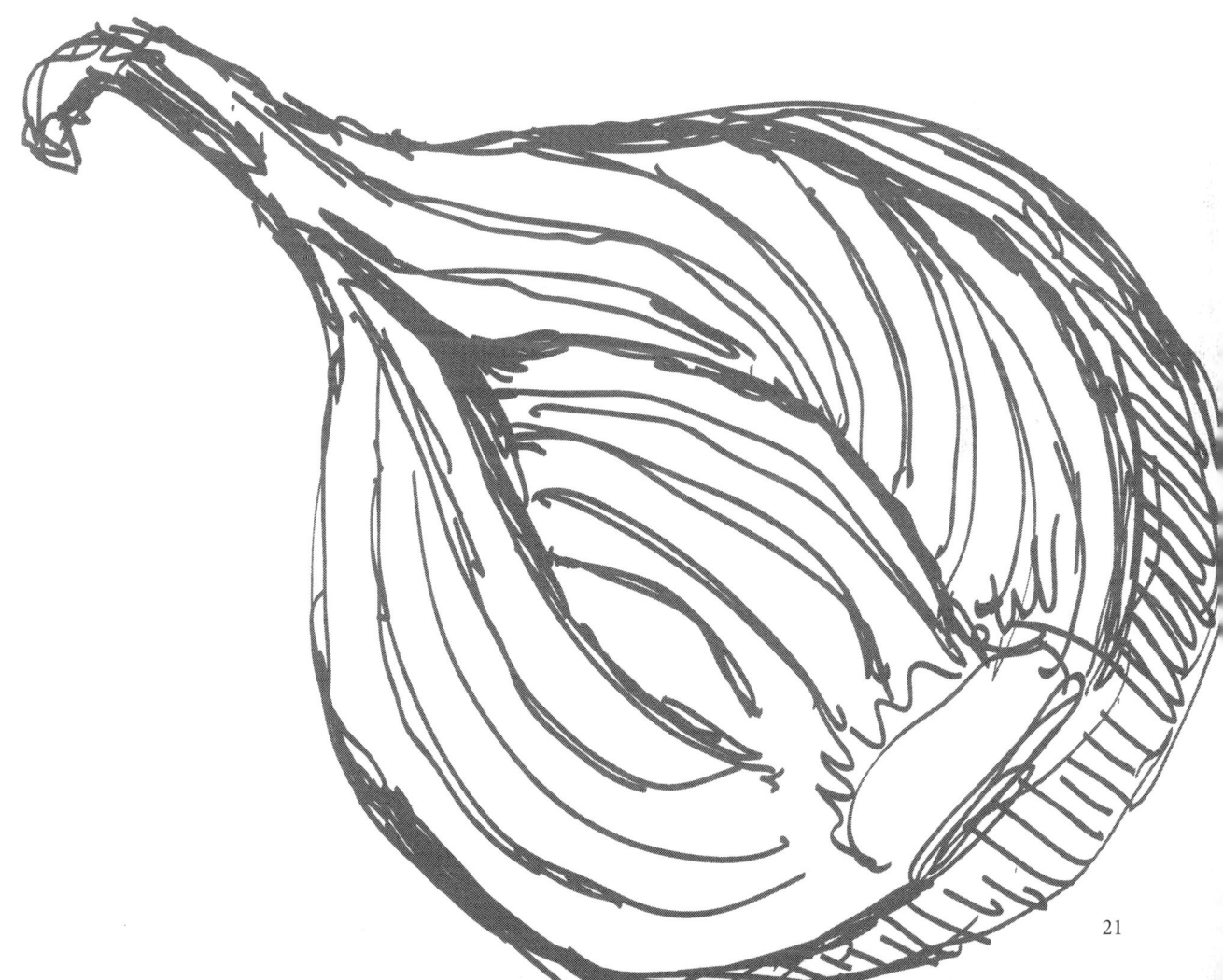

CHICKEN
Biryani

Prep Time: 30 mins
Total Time: 2 hrs 30 mins

Servings per Recipe: 8
Calories   832 kcal
Carbohydrates   78.9 g
Cholesterol   134 mg
Fat   35.1 g
Protein   47.8 g
Sodium   1522 mg

Ingredients

4 tbsps vegetable oil
4 small potatoes, peeled and halved
2 large onions, finely chopped
2 cloves garlic, minced
One tbsp minced fresh ginger root
1/2 tsp chili powder
1/2 tsp ground black pepper
1/2 tsp ground turmeric
One tsp ground cumin
One tsp salt
2 medium tomatoes, peeled and chopped
2 tbsps plain yogurt
2 tbsps chopped fresh mint leaves
1/2 tsp ground cardamom

One (2 inch) piece cinnamon stick
3 pounds boneless, skinless chicken pieces cut into chunks
2 1/2 tbsps vegetable oil
One large onion, diced
One pinch powdered saffron
5 pods cardamom
3 whole cloves
One (One inch) piece cinnamon stick
1/2 tsp ground ginger
One pound basmati rice
4 cups chicken stock
One 1/2 tsps salt

Directions

1. Okay let's begin this recipe by grabbing a frying pan or large skillet and mix in some veggie oil (two tbsps).
2. Once our veggie oil is hot add potatoes and fry them until they are a brownish color.
3. Once the potatoes are brown remove any excess oil and place them to the side for work later.
4. Keep the pan hot and add two more tbsps of oil and add some garlic, onion, and ginger.
5. Cook these contents until you find that your onions are nice and soft and slightly brown.
6. Now we want to add the following ingredients to our onions for seasoning: tomatoes, chili, salt, pepper, cumin, and turmeric.
7. Make sure that you vigorously stir the seasonings to protect them from burning while

frying for about five mins.
8. Now we want to combine the following ingredients: a cinnamon stick, yogurt, cardamom, and mint.
9. Once these ingredients are added we want to place a lid over the pot and lower its heat to the lowest level.
10. Take care to stir the mixture every once and a while until you find that the tomatoes have been turned into a pulp.
11. You may notice that the mixture will become dry and sticky. If this is the case you will need to combine some hot water to the cooking pot occasionally.
12. Once the contents are thick. Grab your chicken pieces and combine them with the sauce.
13. You will want to make sure to mix the chicken well with the sauce so that every piece is evenly coated.
14. You now want to place a lid on the mixture and lower the temperature to its low level.
15. The chicken should be heated at this level while covered until you find that it is tender. Typically this will take about 35 to 45 mins.
16. Cook the chicken down until you notice a bit of gravy left. If you find that the gravy is too much remove the lid from the cooking dish for a while and let the contents continue to cook.
17. Now let's get to the rice.
18. Get your rice and wash it until you find the water running clear. Drain the water with a colander and let the rice sit aside for about thirty mins.
19. Now grab a large frying pan or skillet and add some veggie oil with some onions and fry it up until it is nice and golden.
20. Grab the following ingredients and add them to the onions: rice, saffron, ginger, cardamom, cinnamon stick, and some cloves. Make sure that you stir consistently until you find that your rice is completely covered with spice.
21. Now we need to get another pot of a medium size.
22. Grab some chicken stock as well as some salt.
23. When you find that the rice is nice and hot you want to add this chicken stock and salt to it. Make sure that you combine everything well.
24. Now let's grab that chicken and potato pot from earlier.
25. We want to combine the chicken and potatoes nicely into the rice mixture.
26. Cover the rice pot with a lid and make sure it is completely sealed. We now want to take the temperature down to its lowest level and let this rice simmer for about 20 mins.
27. Make sure that you do not lift the lid while it is cooking.
28. After 20 mins has elapsed remove the lid and fluff the biryani.
29. It is now ready to be plated and served.
30. Enjoy.

BROWN RICE, Chicken, Curry, Casserole

Prep Time: 15 mins
Total Time: 1 hr 15 mins

Servings per Recipe: 4
Calories   241 kcal
Carbohydrates   34.5 g
Cholesterol   50 mg
Fat   2 g
Protein   22.7 g
Sodium   620 mg

Ingredients

One cup water
One (8 ounce) can stewed tomatoes
3/4 cup quick-cooking brown rice
1/2 cup raisins
One tbsp lemon juice
3 tsps curry powder
One cube chicken bouillon
1/2 tsp ground cinnamon
1/4 tsp salt
2 cloves garlic, minced
One bay leaf (optional)
3/4 pound skinless, boneless chicken breast halves - cut into One inch pieces

Directions

1. First we need to get our oven ready. So let's turn it on to 350 degrees Fahrenheit or 175 degrees Celsius for preheating.
2. Now grab a frying pan or skillet and combine the following: bay leaf, water, garlic, stewed tomatoes, salt, brown rice, ground cinnamon, raisins, bouillon, lemon juice, and curry powder.
3. Get everything nice and hot so it is boiling.
4. Once we find our mixture is boiling we want to add chicken to it.
5. Now make sure to stir the chicken into the boiling mixture and then move all of the contents to a baking dish (preferably a casserole dish)
6. Finally we want to place a lid on the baking dish and place it into the oven for about 45 mins. Making sure that we occasionally stir the contents.
7. Eventually we will find that the rice is tender and the chicken is fully cooked. In which case this is ready for plating and enjoyment.

Aloo Matar

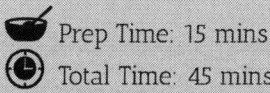
Prep Time: 15 mins
Total Time: 45 mins

Servings per Recipe: 4
Calories   487 kcal
Carbohydrates   81.7 g
Cholesterol   0 mg
Fat   14.5 g
Protein   9 g
Sodium   898 mg

Ingredients

- 1/4 cup vegetable oil
- 2 medium onions, finely chopped
- One tbsp ginger garlic paste
- One bay leaf
- 4 large potatoes, peeled and chopped
- One cup frozen peas
- 1/2 cup tomato puree
- One 1/2 tsps garam masala
- One 1/2 tsps paprika
- One tsp white sugar
- One tsp salt
- 2 tbsps chopped cilantro

Directions

1. Grab a wok and some oil and get them both hot and ready for cooking before going to the next step.
2. Once we have a hot wok grab the following ingredients and add them to the wok: bay leaf, onions, garlic paste, and ginger.
3. Make sure to fry the seasonings while stirring consistently until you find that the onions are translucent.
4. Once the onions are see-through and ready. Combine peas and potatoes with your onions.
5. Place a lid on this pot and let it cook down until the potatoes are soft. Typically this will take about 15 mins.
6. One you find that the potatoes are soft discard the bay leaf.
7. Grab the following ingredients to mix in: salt, tomato puree, sugar, garam masala, and paprika.
8. Combine everything and let it all cook for about 10 minutes.
9. Finally we want to grab some cilantro and throw it in. Let everything go for about another 2 mins and it is ready for serving.
10. Enjoy.

POTATOES
Indian Style

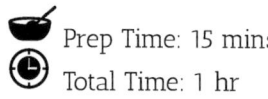

Prep Time: 15 mins
Total Time: 1 hr

Servings per Recipe: 4
Calories	396 kcal
Carbohydrates	64.7 g
Cholesterol	28 mg
Fat	11.3 g
Protein	11.3 g
Sodium	677 mg

Ingredients

- 3 tbsps ghee
- One tsp cumin seeds
- One tsp turmeric
- One tsp ground coriander
- One tsp salt
- 1/2 tsp mustard seed
- 1/2 tsp ground cayenne pepper
- 6 medium potatoes, peeled and diced
- 2 cups water
- One cup yogurt
- 2/3 cup frozen green peas

Directions

1. Grab a frying pan or a skillet and get some veggie oil as well. Place the oil into the pan and place everything over a medium level of heating.
2. Get everything nice and hot and add the following ingredients: cayenne pepper, cumin, mustard seed, turmeric, salt, and coriander.
3. Get your potatoes and put them into the frying pan as well. Be sure to mix everything well and make sure you coat the potatoes with veggie oil or ghee.
4. For about one min make sure you consistently stir everything and let it cook down nicely.
5. After 10 mins of stirring and cooking combine water into the frying pan.
6. After the water has been added lower the heat to its lowest level and let everything simmer for about 30 mins. At which point you should notice your potatoes are soft.
7. Once the potatoes are soft add some yogurt and peas into the mix and make sure everything is heated nicely before cooling.
8. Plate.
9. Enjoy.

Dahl II

🥣 Prep Time: 30 mins
🕐 Total Time: 2 hrs

Servings per Recipe: 6
Calories   209 kcal
Carbohydrates   30.6 g
Cholesterol   0 mg
Fat   5.7 g
Fiber   12.7 g
Protein   10.4 g

Ingredients

- One cup red lentils
- 2 tbsps ginger root, minced
- One tsp mustard seed
- 2 tbsps chopped fresh cilantro
- 4 tomatoes, chopped
- 3 onions, chopped
- 3 jalapeno peppers, seeded and minced
- One tbsp ground cumin
- One tbsp ground coriander seed
- 6 cloves garlic, minced
- 2 tbsps olive oil
- One cup water
- Salt to taste

Directions

1. Before anything we need to get our lentils nice and soft. So grab a pressure cooker and add the lentils.
2. Pressurize them until they are soft. Otherwise cook the lentils in a pot with water (slower method).
3. Grab a frying pan or skillet and get some oil hot with mustard seeds as well.
4. You'll notice the mustard seeds begin to flutter when the oil is very hot. This is what we are looking for.
5. When the mustard seeds are fluttering add the following ingredients: garlic, onions, jalapeno pepper, and ginger.
6. We want to stir fry all these ingredients until both the garlic and onions are nice and brownish. Once the onions are brown and golden add some cumin and coriander to the mix. Continue by adding tomatoes.
7. Stir fry the contents until you notice the tomatoes are done. Add some water at this point.
8. Let the newly added water begin to boil for about six mins.
9. Now we need to combine the cooked lentils with some salt with the boiling mixture.
10. Finally combine some cilantro before serving the dish right off the heat.
11. Enjoy.

OKRA Curry

Prep Time: 20 mins
Total Time: 35 mins

Servings per Recipe: 4
Calories   100 kcal
Carbohydrates   15.8 g
Cholesterol   0 mg
Fat   3.9 g
Protein   3.4 g
Sodium   597 mg

Ingredients

4 cups okra, cut into 1-inch pieces
One tbsp olive oil
One tsp cumin seeds
One onion, chopped
2 tomatoes, diced

One tsp curry powder
One tsp salt

Directions

1. First we need to grab a dish that can be microwaved safely.
2. Grab your okra and put it into this dish, which should be as large as possible.
3. Cook the okra in the microwave for about six mins on its highest setting.
4. Now find a frying pan or skillet and add some cumin seeds and olive oil.
5. The oil and seeds should be placed over a medium level of heat and eventually you'll notice them begin to swell.
6. Once cumin seeds have begun to swell take the onion and begin to fry it.
7. The cooking process of the onion should last for about three mins.
8. After the onions have been cooked grab your tomatoes and add them to the mix.
9. Allow the tomatoes to cook for three more mins.
10. After the tomatoes have cooked for a bit we need to combine our tomatoes with the okra, some salt, and some curry powder.
11. Finally stir the contents for about three mins at which point it is ready for plating.
12. Serve and enjoy.

Lentil, Tomato Soup, Indian Style

Prep Time: 5 mins
Total Time: 30 mins

Servings per Recipe: 2
Calories   239 kcal
Carbohydrates   32 g
Cholesterol   6 mg
Fat   7 g
Protein   12.8 g
Sodium   269 mg

Ingredients

One onion, finely chopped
One tbsp olive oil
One chili pepper, chopped
One cup red lentils
One (14.5 ounce) can peeled and diced tomatoes
One cup water
salt and pepper to taste
1/2 tsp ground cumin
One tsp dried basil
1/4 cup sour cream
2 fresh basil leaves

Directions

1. Grab a pan for heating possibly a Dutch oven. You want to begin heating some olive oil in it.
2. Once you have the oil heated add some onions and cook them down until they are translucent.
3. Once the onions are translucent we want to add the following ingredients: basil, tomatoes, cumin, chili pepper, and lentils with some water.
4. All the contents should be brought to a boil.
5. Once everything is boiling you must lower the heat to a low to medium level and put lentils.
6. Once at the low to medium level let everything simmer nicely for about 20 mins. At this point you will find that the lentils are soft.
7. Now that the lentils are ready we should take a stick blender and mash the soup until it has been nicely pureed. You can now add some salt and pepper if you like but it is not necessary.
8. Serve and enjoy.

INDIAN STYLE
Salsa

Prep Time: 5 mins
Total Time: 1 hr 5 mins

Servings per Recipe: 6
Calories   56 kcal
Carbohydrates   10.5 g
Cholesterol   0 mg
Fat   0.6 g
Protein   1.9 g
Sodium   971 mg

Ingredients

4 cups chopped tomatoes
2 cups green bell pepper, chopped
3/4 cup chopped onion
One cup jalapeno pepper
One 1/2 tsps salt
1/2 tsp minced garlic
One 1/4 cups cider vinegar

Directions

1. Grab the following ingredients and combine them in a nice sized pot: vinegar, bell peppers, garlic, onion, salt, and hot peppers.
2. Heat the contents until it begins to simmer nicely.
3. Once you find that the mixture is simmering place a lid over the pan and let it continue to simmer for about an hour.
4. The longer you allow the salsa to simmer the spicier and tastier it will be.
5. When suited to your taste. Let the mixture cool and serve.
6. Enjoy.

Vegan Classical Indian Style Relish

🥣 Prep Time: 5 mins
🕐 Total Time: 4 hrs 35 mins

Servings per Recipe: 24
Calories   38 kcal
Fat   0.1 g
Carbohydrates   9.6 g
Protein   0.2 g
Cholesterol   0 mg
Sodium   2 mg

Ingredients

2 red bell peppers, chopped
1 sweet onion, peeled and chopped
1 C. apple cider vinegar
1 C. white sugar
1 tbsp crushed red pepper flakes

Directions

1. In a medium pan, mix together the red bell peppers, onion, apple cider vinegar, sugar and crushed red pepper flakes on medium heat band bring to a boil.
2. Reduce the heat and simmer, stirring occasionally for about 30 minutes.
3. Refrigerate for about 4 hours or overnight before serving.

NORTHERN
Indian Chickpeas

Prep Time: 25 mins
Total Time: 45 mins

Servings per Recipe: 6
Calories	232 kcal
Fat	6.5 g
Carbohydrates	36.9 g
Protein	7.9 g
Cholesterol	0 mg
Sodium	542 mg

Ingredients

2 tbsp vegetable oil
4 cloves garlic, minced
1/2 C. onion, chopped
1 tbsp minced fresh ginger root
1/8 tsp garam masala
2 tsp channa masala spice mix
1 large tomato, chopped
1 1/2 C. water
2 (15.5 oz.) cans garbanzo beans, drained and rinsed
salt to taste

Directions

1. In a pan, heat the oil on medium-high heat and sauté the onion, garlic and ginger till browned.
2. Stir in the garam masala, channa masala spice, tomato, water, garbanzo beans and salt and bring to a simmer.
3. Reduce the heat to low and simmer, covered for about 20 minutes.

Sabji (Traditional Spiced Vegetables)

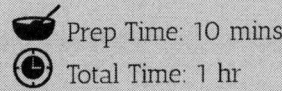

Prep Time: 10 mins
Total Time: 1 hr

Servings per Recipe: 4
Calories	204 kcal
Fat	7.9 g
Carbohydrates	29 g
Protein	4.7 g
Cholesterol	0 mg
Sodium	749 mg

Ingredients

- 2 tbsp canola oil
- 1 tsp cumin seeds
- 1 tsp mustard seed
- 1 tbsp ground coriander
- 1/2 tsp ground turmeric
- 1/2 tsp red chili powder
- 1/2 head cabbage, sliced
- 2 potatoes, chopped
- 1 tbsp ginger-garlic paste
- 1 tsp salt
- 1/2 C. water, or as needed
- 1/4 C. chopped fresh cilantro

Directions

1. In a wok, heat the oil on medium-high heat and sauté the cumin and mustard seeds for about 1-2 minutes.
2. Add the coriander, turmeric and cayenne pepper and sauté for about 1 minute.
3. Stir in the cabbage, potatoes, ginger-garlic paste and salt.
4. Add enough water to steam the vegetables.
5. Cook, covered for about 45 minutes, stirring occasionally and adding more water if needed.
6. Remove from the heat and serve with a garnishing of the cilantro.

TACOS
Indian Style

🥣 Prep Time: 20 mins
⏱ Total Time: 40 mins

Servings per Recipe: 6
Calories   696 kcal
Fat   40.9 g
Carbohydrates   50.5g
Protein   32.6 g
Cholesterol   103 mg
Sodium   1371 mg

Ingredients

2 C. all-purpose flour
1 tbsp baking powder
1/2 tsp white sugar
1/2 tsp salt
1 1/2 C. lukewarm water
2 C. oil for frying
1 lb. ground beef

1 (1.25 oz.) package chili seasoning mix
1 (15 oz.) can kidney beans, drained
2 C. shredded Cheddar cheese
2 C. chopped iceberg lettuce
2 tomatoes, chopped
1 C. sour cream

Directions

1. In a large bowl, mix together the flour, baking powder, sugar and salt.
2. Add the water and stir till a sticky dough forms and keep aside to rest while the oil is heating.
3. In a deep fryer, heat the oil to 375 degrees F.
4. Divide the dough into 6 equal portions and flatten each portion into a circle about the size of your palm.
5. Add the dough circles, one at a time in hot oil and fry for about 2 minutes.
6. With tongs, change the side and cook for about 1 minute more.
7. Transfer onto a paper towel lined plate to drain.
8. Heat a large skillet on medium heat and cook the beef till browned completely.
9. Stir in the chili seasoning and kidney beans and cook for about 5 minutes.
10. Place fry bread on a plate and top each with the chili mixture, followed by the shredded Cheddar cheese, lettuce, tomatoes and sour cream.

Tandoori Pizza

Prep Time: 20 mins
Total Time: 9 hrs

Servings per Recipe: 4
Calories	1058 kcal
Fat	65.8 g
Carbohydrates	164g
Protein	53.7 g
Cholesterol	1159 mg
Sodium	2444 mg

Ingredients

- 1/2 C. tandoori paste
- 6 tbsp plain yogurt
- 2 skinless, boneless chicken breast halves
- 6 tbsp olive oil, divided
- 4 pieces tandoori naan bread
- 3 tsp spicy curry powder
- 1 tsp ground turmeric
- 1 yellow bell pepper, thinly sliced
- 1 large red onion, thinly sliced
- 4 (4 oz.) spreadable goat cheese
- 1 tomato, thinly sliced
- 4 oz. feta cheese

Directions

1. In a large bowl, add the tandoori paste and yogurt and beat till well combined.
2. Add the chicken and toss to coat well.
3. With the plastic wrap, cover and refrigerate to marinate for about 8 hours or overnight.
4. Set your oven to 425 degrees F.
5. In a large skillet, heat 1 tbsp of the olive oil on medium-high heat.
6. Remove the chicken from the marinade and shake off any excess marinade.
7. Add the chicken breasts in hot oil and cook, flipping occasionally for about 10-12 minutes. Transfer the chicken into a bowl and with 2 forks, shred it.
8. Brush each piece of naan with about 1 tsp olive oil and sprinkle with a pinch of curry powder and place naan on a baking sheet.
9. Cook in the oven for about 5 minutes.
10. In a skillet, heat the remaining olive oil on medium-high heat and stir fry the yellow pepper, onion, 2 tsp of the curry powder and turmeric for about 5-7 minutes.
11. Place the goat cheese over each naan piece evenly and sprinkle with the curry powder.
12. Top each naan piece with the shredded chicken, followed by pepper mixture, tomato and feta cheese.
13. Sprinkle with a pinch of curry powder and cook in the oven for about 20 minutes.

SOUTH INDIAN STYLE
Crepes

🥣 Prep Time: 10 mins
🕐 Total Time: 30 mins

Servings per Recipe: 6
Calories   125 kcal
Fat   5 g
Carbohydrates   16.5g
Protein   3.5 g
Cholesterol   41 mg
Sodium   41 mg

Ingredients

1 C. all-purpose flour
1 C. water
1 egg
2 tbsp butter, melted

1 pinch salt
1 tbsp caraway seeds

Directions

1. Heat a non-stick crepe pan on medium-high heat.
2. In a bowl, add the flour and water and beat well.
3. Add the egg and mix well.
4. Add the butter, salt and caraway seeds and beat till a smooth mixture forms.
5. Add about 1/4 C. of the mixture in the heated pan and tilt the pan to spread the mixture evenly.
6. Cook for about 2-4 minutes.
7. Carefully, flip the crepe and cook for about 30 seconds.
8. Repeat with the remaining mixture.

Lassi (Popular Yogurt Drink)

Prep Time: 15 mins
Total Time: 15 mins

Servings per Recipe: 6	
Calories	50 kcal
Fat	1.1 g
Cholesterol	6.4g
Sodium	3.8 g
Carbohydrates	4 mg
Protein	51 mg

Ingredients

- 1 3/4 C. plain yogurt
- 6 cubes ice, crushed
- 1 1/2 C. ice water
- 2 tsp white sugar
- 1 pinch salt

Directions

1. In a blender, add all the ingredients and pulse till frothy.
2. In tall glasses, place the ice cubes and pour the blended mixture over the ice and serve.

KOLKATA STYLE
Pudding

🥣 Prep Time: 20 mins
🕐 Total Time: 1 hr 50 mins

Servings per Recipe: 5
Calories   386 kcal
Fat   14.2 g
Carbohydrates   57.9 g
Protein   8.7 g
Cholesterol   42 mg
Sodium   638 mg

Ingredients

4 1/2 C. milk
2/3 C. cornmeal
1/4 C. butter
1/2 C. dark molasses
1 tsp salt
1/4 C. white sugar
1 tsp ground cinnamon

Directions

1. Set your oven to 325 degrees F before doing anything else and grease a large baking dish.
2. Add about 3 1/2 C. of the milk in top of double boiler over direct heat and heat it.
3. Remove the milk from the heat.
4. In a bowl, mix together the cornmeal with the remaining 1 C. of the milk.
5. Add the cornmeal mixture into the scalding milk, stirring continuously.
6. Place the milk mixture into the top of the double boiler and cook for about 20 minutes, stirring occasionally.
7. Stir in the butter, molasses, salt, sugar and cinnamon and transfer the mixture into the prepared baking dish.
8. Cook in the oven for about 1 1/2 hours.

A Fruity Salad in Indian

Prep Time: 15 mins
Total Time: 35 mins

Servings per Recipe: 4
Calories	451 kcal
Fat	13.7 g
Carbohydrates	76.9 g
Protein	8.3 g
Cholesterol	41 mg
Sodium	218 mg

Ingredients

- 1 1/2 C. brown rice
- 4 C. water
- 1 (10 oz.) can asparagus tips, drained
- 1 red bell pepper, seeded and diced
- 2 red apples, cored and diced
- 1/4 C. golden raisins
- 1/2 C. heavy cream
- 1 tsp curry powder
- 1 tsp lemon juice
- salt and pepper to taste

Directions

1. In a pan, add the rice and water and bring to a boil.
2. Reduce the heat to low and simmer, covered for about 30 minutes.
3. Drain, if necessary and keep aside to cool.
4. Meanwhile in a bowl, place the golden raisins and fill with enough hot water to cover and keep aside for about 20 minutes to plump.
5. Drain well.
6. In a medium bowl, add the cream and beat till soft peaks form.
7. Fold in the curry powder, lemon juice, salt and pepper.
8. In another bowl, mix together the brown rice, asparagus, red pepper, apples and raisins.
9. Fold into the curry cream and refrigerate to chill till serving.

AUTHENTIC Saag (Tasty Spiced Greens)

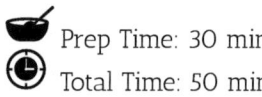 Prep Time: 30 mins
Total Time: 50 mins

Servings per Recipe: 6
Calories   182 kcal
Fat   16.2 g
Carbohydrates   7.6g
Protein   4.7 g
Cholesterol   41 mg
Sodium   565 mg

Ingredients

- 1/2 C. butter
- 2 tsp cumin seed
- 1 green chili pepper, seeded and diced
- 2 cloves garlic, chopped
- 2 tbsp ground turmeric
- 1 lb. chopped fresh mustard greens
- 1 lb. chopped fresh spinach
- 1 tsp ground cumin
- 1 tsp ground coriander
- 1 tsp salt

Directions

1. In a large skillet, melt the butter on medium-high heat and cook and sauté the cumin seed, chili pepper, garlic and turmeric for about 2 minutes.
2. Stir in the chopped mustard greens and spinach a little at a time, adding the stems and thicker leaves.
3. Slowly, add greens and cook till all the greens have been added and all are completely wilted.
4. Stir in the cumin, coriander, and salt.
5. Reduce the heat and simmer for about 10 minutes, adding water as needed to keep the greens moist.

Spicy Masala Cauliflower

Prep Time: 10 mins
Total Time: 50 mins

Servings per Recipe: 5
Calories   168 kcal
Fat   11.6 g
Carbohydrates   15.1g
Protein   4.6 g
Cholesterol   0 mg
Sodium   62 mg

Ingredients

- 1 large head cauliflower
- 4 tbsp vegetable oil
- 1/2 tsp ground turmeric
- 1 small onion, minced
- 2 tomatoes, pureed
- 1 tsp garlic powder
- 3 tsp garam masala (optional)
- salt to taste
- 1/2 head lettuce

Directions

1. Set your oven to 350 degrees F before doing anything else.
2. Cut off most of the cauliflower's stem and arrange the whole head in a baking dish.
3. In a small frying pan, heat 2 tbsp of the oil and turmeric.
4. Coat the cauliflower head with the turmeric oil evenly.
5. Cook in the oven for about 30 minutes.
6. Meanwhile in a frying pan, heat 2 tbsp of the oil and sauté the minced onions till a medium brown color forms.
7. Add the pureed tomatoes, garlic powder, garam masala and salt and simmer for about 10 minutes.
8. In a serving plate, arrange the lettuce leaves and top with the cauliflower on top.
9. Place the tomato curry over the cauliflower and serve hot.

HOMEMADE
Makhani

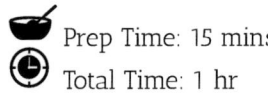
Prep Time: 15 mins
Total Time: 1 hr

Servings per Recipe: 6
Calories	880 kcal
Fat	82.3 g
Carbohydrates	112.8g
Protein	26.4 g
Cholesterol	303 mg
Sodium	11461 mg

Ingredients

1 C. butter, divided
1 onion, minced
1 tbsp minced garlic
1 (15 oz.) can tomato sauce
3 C. heavy cream
2 tsp salt
1 tsp cayenne pepper
1 tsp garam masala
1 1/2 lb. skinless, boneless chicken breast, cut into bite-sized chunks
2 tbsp vegetable oil
2 tbsp tandoori masala

Directions

1. Set your oven to 375 degrees F before doing anything else.
2. In a skillet, melt a few tbsp of the butter on medium heat and sauté the onion and garlic for about 15 minutes.
3. Meanwhile melt the remaining butter in a pan on medium-high heat.
4. Add the tomato sauce, heavy cream, salt, cayenne pepper and garam masala and bring to a simmer.
5. Reduce the heat to medium-low and simmer, covered for about 30 minutes, stirring occasionally.
6. Stir in the caramelized onions.
7. Meanwhile in a bowl, add the cubed chicken breast, vegetable oil, tandoori masala and toss to coat.
8. Place the chicken cubes onto a baking sheet in a single layer.
9. Cook in the oven for about 12 minutes.
10. Transfer the chicken into the sauce and simmer for about 5 minutes before serving.

Kebabs
From Mumbai

Prep Time: 15 mins
Total Time: 2 hrs 25 mins

Servings per Recipe: 8
Calories	304 kcal
Fat	22.6 g
Carbohydrates	4.7g
Protein	20.1 g
Cholesterol	76 mg
Sodium	665 mg

Ingredients

- 2 lb. lean ground lamb
- 2 onions, finely chopped
- 1/2 C. fresh mint leaves, finely chopped
- 1/2 C. cilantro, finely chopped
- 1 tbsp ginger paste
- 1 tbsp green chili paste
- 2 tsp ground cumin
- 2 tsp ground coriander
- 2 tsp paprika
- 1 tsp cayenne pepper
- 2 tsp salt
- 1/4 C. vegetable oil
- skewers

Directions

1. In a large bowl, add the ground lamb, onions, mint, cilantro, ginger paste, chili paste, cumin, coriander, paprika, cayenne and salt and mix till well combined.
2. Refrigerate, covered for 2 about hours.
3. Mold about 1 C. of the lamb mixture around the skewers to form the sausages.
4. Refrigerate until you are ready to grill.
5. Set your grill for high heat and grease the grill grate.
6. Cook the sausages on the grill for about 10 minutes, flipping occasionally.

GINGER
Coconut Curry Chicken

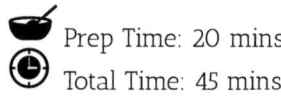
Prep Time: 20 mins
Total Time: 45 mins

Servings per Recipe: 4
Calories	313 kcal
Fat	21.7 g
Carbohydrates	14g
Protein	19.1 g
Cholesterol	38 mg
Sodium	268 mg

Ingredients

3 tbsp olive oil
1 small onion, chopped
2 cloves garlic, minced
3 tbsp curry powder
1 tsp ground cinnamon
1 tsp paprika
1 bay leaf
1/2 tsp grated fresh ginger root
1/2 tsp white sugar
salt to taste
2 skinless, boneless chicken breast halves - cut into bite-size pieces
1 tbsp tomato paste
1 C. plain yogurt
3/4 C. coconut milk
1/2 lemon, juiced
1/2 tsp cayenne pepper

Directions

1. In a skillet, heat the olive oil on medium heat and sauté the onion till golden brown.
2. Stir in the garlic, curry powder, cinnamon, paprika, bay leaf, ginger, sugar and salt and sauté for about 2 minutes.
3. Add the chicken pieces, tomato paste, yogurt and coconut milk and bring to a boil.
4. Reduce the heat and simmer for about 20-25 minutes.
5. Discard the bay leaf and stir in the lemon juice and cayenne pepper.
6. Simmer for about 5 minutes.

An Indian Breakfast Cereal

Prep Time: 15 mins
Total Time: 15 mins

Servings per Recipe: 22
Calories	147 kcal
Fat	6.7 g
Cholesterol	20g
Sodium	3.4 g
Carbohydrates	2 mg
Protein	266 mg

Ingredients

- 3 C. Rice Chex(R) cereal
- 3 C. Corn Chex(R) cereal
- 3 C. Wheat Chex(R) cereal
- 1 C. cashews
- 1/2 C. pistachios (shelled)
- 1/2 C. almonds
- 1 1/2 tbsp butter
- 3 tbsp light corn syrup
- 3 tbsp honey
- 3/4 tsp salt
- 3/4 tsp ground cardamom
- 1/2 tsp ground ginger
- Dash cayenne pepper

Directions

1. In a large microwave safe bowl, mix together the cereals, cashews, pistachios, and almonds.
2. In another small microwave safe bowl add the butter and microwave on High for about 30 seconds.
3. Stir in the corn syrup and honey and microwave on High for about 10 seconds.
4. Add salt, cardamom, ginger, and cayenne and stir to combine well.
5. Place the butter mixture over the cereal mixture and stir till well combined.
6. Microwave the mixture on High for about 3 minutes, stirring after every 1 minute.
7. Spread onto a foil paper to cool.
8. Store in airtight container.

STANDARD
Oven Roasted Samosas

Prep Time: 30 mins
Total Time: 1 hr 40 mins

Servings per Recipe: 16
Calories   315 kcal
Fat   18.7 g
Carbohydrates   32.7g
Protein   4.9 g
Cholesterol   0 mg
Sodium   396 mg

Ingredients

4 potatoes, peeled and cubed
1/4 C. oil
2 small onions, finely chopped
3 tbsp coriander seed
1 tbsp curry powder
1 (1 inch) piece fresh ginger, grated
1 tsp salt
1 tsp ground turmeric
1 tsp ground cumin
1/2 tsp ground allspice
1/2 tsp cayenne pepper
1/8 tsp ground cinnamon
2 roma (plum) tomatoes, finely chopped
1/2 C. frozen peas
4 prepared pie crusts
2 egg whites, beaten, or as needed

Directions

1. In a large pan of salted water, add the potatoes and bring to a boil.
2. Reduce heat to medium-low and simmer for about 20 minutes.
3. Drain and transfer potatoes to a bowl.
4. With a fork, mash the potatoes roughly.
5. Set your oven to 400 degrees F.
6. In a skillet, heat the oil on medium-high heat and sauté the onions, coriander seed, curry powder, ginger, salt, turmeric, cumin, allspice, cayenne pepper and cinnamon for about 5 minutes. Remove from the heat and stir in the tomatoes and pea.
7. Transfer the peas mixture into mashed potatoes and mix well.
8. Keep aside to cool completely. Cut each pie crust into 8 even triangles.
9. Place the filling onto the wide end of each triangle and fold corners over the filling creating a triangular 'hat' shape.
10. Pinch the dough together to seal and brush the egg white over each samosa.
11. Arrange samosas on a baking sheet.
12. Cook in the oven for about 15 minutes.

Curry Russets Indian Style

Prep Time: 10 mins
Total Time: 30 mins

Servings per Recipe: 5
Calories	268 kcal
Fat	4.7 g
Carbohydrates	52.1g
Protein	6.3 g
Cholesterol	0 mg
Sodium	267 mg

Ingredients

- 1 C. vegetable oil for frying
- 2 cloves garlic, pressed
- 1 tsp cumin seeds
- 1/2 tsp salt
- 1/4 tsp ground turmeric
- 1/4 tsp ground black pepper
- 5 russet potatoes, peeled and cubed
- 2 tbsp chopped fresh cilantro
- 1 tsp mild curry paste

Directions

1. In a frying pan, add the enough oil to cover the bottom 1/3-inch deep on medium heat.
2. Add the garlic, cumin, salt, turmeric and black pepper and heat it.
3. Stir in the potatoes and cook for about 10-15 minutes, flipping occasionally.
4. Stir in the fresh cilantro and curry paste and stir fry for about 1 minute.
5. With a slotted spoon, transfer the potatoes into serving dish.

CHAI
for Chatting

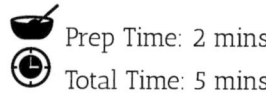

Prep Time: 2 mins
Total Time: 5 mins

Servings per Recipe: 1
Calories	126 kcal
Fat	3 g
Carbohydrates	19.3g
Protein	5.1 g
Cholesterol	10 mg
Sodium	131 mg

Ingredients

1/2 C. water
1/2 C. milk
1 chai tea bag
1 (.55 oz.) package instant hot chocolate mix

Directions

1. In a microwave-safe mug, mix together the water and milk and microwave on High for about 1 1/2 minutes.
2. Remove and add the chai teabag and keep aside to steep for about 2 minutes.
3. Discard the tea bag, and stir in the hot chocolate mix.

Basmaati Rice 101

Prep Time: 10 mins
Total Time: 45 mins

Servings per Recipe: 6
Calories	216 kcal
Fat	5.4 g
Carbohydrates	38.9 g
Protein	3.9 g
Cholesterol	0 mg
Sodium	394 mg

Ingredients

- 1 1/2 C. basmati rice
- 2 tbsp vegetable oil
- 1 (2 inch) piece cinnamon stick
- 2 pods green cardamom
- 2 whole cloves
- 1 tbsp cumin seed
- 1 tsp salt
- 2 1/2 C. water
- 1 small onion, thinly sliced

Directions

1. In a bowl, place the rice and enough water to cover.
2. Keep aside for about 20 minutes.
3. In a large pan, heat the oil on medium heat and sauté the cinnamon stick, cardamom pods, cloves and cumin seed for about 1 minute.
4. Stir in the onion and sauté for about 10 minutes.
5. Drain the water from the rice and stir into the pan.
6. Stir fry the rice for a few minutes or till lightly toasted.
7. Add the salt and water and bring to a boil.
8. Reduce the heat to low and simmer, covered for about 15 minutes.
9. Remove from the heat and keep aside for about 5 minutes.
10. With a fork, fluff the rice before serving.

SPICY Beef Roast Hyderabadi Inspired

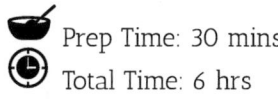

Prep Time: 30 mins
Total Time: 6 hrs

Servings per Recipe: 12
Calories   271 kcal
Fat   18.4 g
Carbohydrates   7.6 g
Protein   18.7 g
Cholesterol   69 mg
Sodium   172 mg

Ingredients

1 (4 lb.) boneless beef chuck roast
3 cloves garlic, crushed
1 (1 inch) piece ginger, crushed
3 dried red chilies, broken
3 whole black peppercorns, coarsely crushed
3 whole cloves
1 (1 inch) piece cinnamon stick
1/2 tsp cumin seeds
1/2 tsp ground coriander
salt to taste
3 C. water
1 tbsp vegetable oil
2 onions, sliced
1/2 tsp chili powder
2 large tomatoes, chopped
1/2 C. ketchup
2 tbsp tomato puree
1 tsp ground black pepper
2 tbsp chopped fresh cilantro

Directions

1. In a slow cooker, mix together the chuck roast, garlic, ginger, chilies, peppercorns, cloves, cinnamon stick, cumin, coriander, salt and water.
2. Set the slow cooker on High and cook, covered for about 4-6 hours.
3. Transfer the roast into a bowl and keep aside to cool slightly.
4. Cut the roast into thick slices.
5. Strain the liquid, reserving in a bowl and discard the spices.
6. Set your oven to 350 degrees F.
7. In a large oven-proof skillet, heat the oil on medium heat and sauté the onion for about 5-7 minutes.
8. Sprinkle the chili powder over onions and sauté for about 30 seconds.
9. Stir in the tomatoes, ketchup, tomato puree, black pepper and reserved cooking liquid and cook for about 10 minutes and mixture reduced to 3 C.

10. Stir in the sliced meat and simmer for about 5-10 minutes.
11. Transfer the skillet into the oven and cook for about 10-15 minutes, basting occasionally with the sauce.
12. Serve with a garnishing of the chopped cilantro.

KERALA
Curry

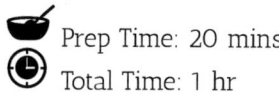
Prep Time: 20 mins
Total Time: 1 hr

Servings per Recipe: 8
Calories   542 kcal
Fat   39.3 g
Carbohydrates   29.7g
Protein   18.4 g
Cholesterol   60 mg
Sodium   66 mg

Ingredients

- 1 (3 lb.) chicken, cut into pieces
- 1/4 C. vegetable oil
- 2 onions, chopped
- 8 cloves garlic, chopped
- 1/4 C. mild curry powder
- 2 tbsp hot curry powder
- 1 tsp ground black pepper
- salt to taste
- 5 russet potatoes, peeled and cut into 1-inch pieces

Directions

1. In a large pan, add the chicken and enough water to cover and bring to a boil.
2. Reduce the heat to medium and simmer for about 20 minutes.
3. Meanwhile in a large skillet, heat the vegetable oil on medium heat and sauté the onion and garlic for about 5 minutes.
4. Stir in both curry powders, black pepper and salt and sauté for about 5 minutes.
5. Transfer the onion mixture into the pan with the chicken.
6. Stir in the potatoes and simmer for about 20 minutes.

Southern Coconut Curry

Prep Time: 25 mins
Total Time: 1 hr

Servings per Recipe: 4
Calories   409 kcal
Fat   28.4 g
Carbohydrates   18.3g
Protein   23.1 g
Cholesterol   69 mg
Sodium   868 mg

Ingredients

- 2 tsp curry powder
- 1 tsp curry paste, see appendix
- 1 (13.5 oz.) can coconut milk
- 2 tbsp fish sauce
- 1 tbsp packed brown sugar
- 1 C. chicken stock
- 4 chicken thighs, cut into bite size pieces
- 1/2 C. frozen peas
- 1/2 C. chopped green bell pepper
- 1/2 C. chopped carrot
- 1 tbsp cornstarch
- 2 tbsp chicken stock
- 3/4 C. chopped fresh pineapple

Directions

1. Heat a pan on medium-low heat and sauté the curry powder and curry paste for about 2 minutes.
2. Stir in the coconut milk, fish sauce, brown sugar, and 1 C. of the chicken stock and increase the heat to medium-high.
3. Add the chicken thighs, peas, peppers and carrots and bring to a boil.
4. Reduce the heat to low and simmer for about 25 minutes.
5. In a small bowl, dissolve 1 tbsp of the cornstarch in 2 tbsp of the cold chicken stock.
6. Add the cornstarch mixture into the curry, stirring continuously.
7. Stir in the pineapple and simmer for about 5 minutes

PRIYANKA'S Butter Chicken (Murgh Makhani)

Prep Time: 15 mins
Total Time: 1 hr 10 mins

Servings per Recipe:	4
Calories	659 kcal
Fat	43 g
Carbohydrates	34.3g
Protein	37.2 g
Cholesterol	189 mg
Sodium	1507 mg

Ingredients

2 tsp dried red chili pepper, crushed
1/4 tsp ground cinnamon
1/4 tsp ground nutmeg
1/4 tsp ground cloves
1 1/2 tsp garam masala
1 1/2 tsp salt
1 1/2 tsp minced ginger
2 cloves garlic, crushed
5 Roma tomatoes, seeded, diced
1/2 C. plain yogurt

1 lb. skinless, boneless chicken breast, cut into 2-inch cubes
1/2 C. butter
2 red bell peppers, sliced
2 onions, thinly sliced
1/4 C. heavy whipping cream
2 tbsp chopped fresh coriander

Directions

1. In a large bowl, add the ground red chili peppers, cinnamon, nutmeg, cloves, garam masala, salt, ginger, garlic, tomatoes and yogurt and mix till well combined.
2. Add the chicken cubes and coat with the mixture generously.
3. Refrigerate to marinate for about 30-60 minutes.
4. In a large skillet, melt the butter on medium heat and cook the bell pepper slices and onion until the onion for about 5-7 minutes, stirring occasionally.
5. Add the chicken with the marinade and cook for about 5-10 minutes, stirring continuously.
6. Increase the heat to medium-high and stir in the cream and coriander.
7. Bring to boil, stirring continuously and remove from the heat.
8. Serve immediately.

Anglo-Indian Curry

Prep Time: 30 mins
Total Time: 1 hr

Servings per Recipe: 4
Calories   240 kcal
Fat   9.9 g
Carbohydrates   14.1 g
Protein   24.6 g
Cholesterol   59 mg
Sodium   62 mg

Ingredients

- 2 tbsp vegetable oil
- 1 tsp cumin seed
- 2 medium onions, finely chopped
- 1 tsp ground turmeric
- 1 tsp cayenne pepper
- 1 tsp garam masala, see appendix
- 1 clove garlic, minced
- 1 tbsp minced ginger
- 5 peeled, seeded, and chopped tomatoes
- 1 lb. skinless, boneless chicken breast meat - cubed

Directions

1. In a large pan, heat the oil on medium heat and sauté the cumin seed for about 20-45 seconds.
2. Stir in the onion and sauté for about 5 minutes.
3. Stir in the turmeric, cayenne, garam masala, garlic, and ginger and sauté for about 1-2 minutes.
4. Remove from the heat and keep aside to cool slightly.
5. In a blender, add the onion mixture and tomatoes and pulse till smooth.
6. In the same pan, add the pureed mixture and chicken and gently, simmer for about 20 minutes. (You can add the water to acquire the consistency of your choice.)

CURRIED Chicken Breasts

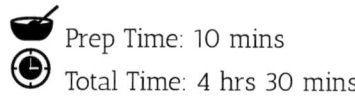
Prep Time: 10 mins
Total Time: 4 hrs 30 mins

Servings per Recipe: 4
Calories 374 kcal
Fat 17.1 g
Carbohydrates 27.6 g
Protein 27.8 g
Cholesterol 109 mg
Sodium 563 mg

Ingredients

- 1/3 C. butter, melted
- 1/3 C. honey
- 1/4 C. Dijon-style prepared mustard
- 4 tsp curry powder
- 1 pinch ground cayenne pepper
- 4 skinless, boneless chicken breasts

Directions

1. In a bowl, add the melted butter, honey, mustard, curry powder and cayenne powder and mix till well combined.
2. Arrange the chicken breasts in a 13x9-inch baking dish and top with the honey mixture evenly.
3. Refrigerate, covered for at least 4 hours to overnight.
4. Set your oven to 375 degrees F.
5. Remove the baking dish from the refrigerator and cook in the oven, covered for about 10 minutes.
6. Uncover and cook in the oven for about 10 minutes more.

Manhattan Restaurant Indian Curry

Prep Time: 20 mins
Total Time: 45 mins

Servings per Recipe: 4
Calories   313 kcal
Fat   21.7 g
Carbohydrates   14g
Protein   19.1 g
Cholesterol   38 mg
Sodium   268 mg

Ingredients

3 tbsp olive oil
1 small onion, chopped
2 cloves garlic, minced
3 tbsp curry powder
1 tsp ground cinnamon
1 tsp paprika
1 bay leaf
1/2 tsp grated fresh ginger root
1/2 tsp white sugar
salt to taste

2 skinless, boneless chicken breast halves - cut into bite-size pieces
1 tbsp tomato paste
1 C. plain yogurt
3/4 C. coconut milk
1/2 lemon, juiced
1/2 tsp cayenne pepper

Directions

1. In a large skillet, heat the olive oil on medium heat and sauté the onion till browned.
2. Stir in the garlic, curry powder, cinnamon, paprika, bay leaf, ginger, sugar and salt and sauté for about 2 minutes.
3. Add the chicken pieces, tomato paste, yogurt and coconut milk and bring to a boil.
4. Reduce the heat and simmer for about 20-25 minutes.
5. Discard the bay leaf and stir in lemon juice and cayenne pepper.
6. Simmer for about 5 minutes.
7. Serve hot.

CARIBBEAN
Coconut Curry

Prep Time: 20 mins
Total Time: 1 hr 10 mins

Servings per Recipe: 6
Calories	375 kcal
Fat	20.9 g
Carbohydrates	16.7g
Protein	32.2 g
Cholesterol	78 mg
Sodium	807 mg

Ingredients

2 lb. boneless skinless chicken breasts, cut into 1/2-inch chunks
1 tsp salt and pepper, or to taste
1 1/2 tbsp vegetable oil
2 tbsp curry powder
1/2 onion, thinly sliced
2 cloves garlic, crushed
1 (14 oz.) can coconut milk
1 (14.5 oz.) can stewed, diced tomatoes
1 (8 oz.) can tomato sauce
3 tbsp sugar

Directions

1. Season the chicken pieces with the salt and pepper evenly.
2. In a large skillet, heat the oil and curry powder on medium-high heat for about 2 minutes.
3. Stir in the onions and garlic and sauté for about 1 minute.
4. Add the chicken and gently, stir to combine with the curry oil.
5. Reduce the heat to medium and cook for about 7-10 minutes.
6. Stir in the coconut milk, tomatoes, tomato sauce and sugar and simmer, covered for about 30-40 minutes, stirring occasionally.

North Indian Inspired Curry

Prep Time: 20 mins
Total Time: 1 hr

Servings per Recipe: 6
Calories	427 kcal
Fat	24.3 g
Carbohydrates	14.7 g
Protein	38.1 g
Cholesterol	95 mg
Sodium	1370 mg

Ingredients

- 2 lb. skinless, boneless chicken breast halves
- 2 tsp salt
- 1/2 C. cooking oil
- 1 1/2 C. chopped onion
- 1 tbsp minced garlic
- 1 1/2 tsp minced fresh ginger root
- 1 tbsp curry powder
- 1 tsp ground cumin
- 1 tsp ground turmeric
- 1 tsp ground coriander
- 1 tsp cayenne pepper
- 1 tbsp water
- 1 (15 oz.) can crushed tomatoes
- 1 C. plain yogurt
- 1 tbsp chopped fresh cilantro
- 1 tsp salt
- 1/2 C. water
- 1 tsp garam masala
- 1 tbsp chopped fresh cilantro
- 1 tbsp fresh lemon juice

Directions

1. Season the chicken breasts with 2 tsp of the salt.
2. In a large skillet, heat the oil on high heat and cook the chicken breasts in the batches till browned completely.
3. Transfer the chicken breasts into a plate and keep aside.
4. In the same skillet, cook the onion, garlic and ginger on medium-high heat for about 8 minutes.
5. Stir in the curry powder, cumin, turmeric, coriander, cayenne and 1 tbsp of the water and sauté for about 1 minute.
6. Stir in the tomatoes, yogurt, and 1 tbsp of the chopped cilantro and 1 tsp of the salt.
7. Add the cooked chicken breasts and 1/2 C. of the water and bring to a boil, turning the chicken occasionally to coat with the sauce.
8. Sprinkle the garam masala and 1 tbsp of the cilantro over the chicken and simmer, covered for about 20 minutes. Serve with a drizzling of the lemon juice.

HOW TO Make Tikka Masala

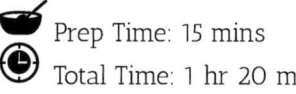

Prep Time: 15 mins
Total Time: 1 hr 20 mins

Servings per Recipe: 6
Calories   328 kcal
Fat   23.4 g
Carbohydrates   13.2g
Protein   17.9 g
Cholesterol   106 mg
Sodium   980 mg

Ingredients

- 2 tbsp ghee (clarified butter)
- 1 onion, finely chopped
- 4 cloves garlic, minced
- 1 tbsp ground cumin
- 1 tsp salt
- 1 tsp ground ginger
- 1 tsp cayenne pepper
- 1/2 tsp ground cinnamon
- 1/4 tsp ground turmeric
- 1 (14 oz.) can tomato sauce
- 1 C. heavy whipping cream
- 2 tsp paprika
- 1 tbsp white sugar
- 1 tbsp vegetable oil
- 4 skinless, boneless chicken breast halves, cut into bite-size pieces
- 1/2 tsp curry powder
- 1/2 tsp salt (optional)
- 1 tsp white sugar (optional)

Directions

1. In a large skillet, melt the ghee on medium heat and sauté the onion for about 5 minutes.
2. Stir in the garlic and sauté about 1 minute.
3. Stir in the cumin, 1 tsp of the salt, ginger, cayenne pepper, cinnamon and turmeric and sauté for about 2 minutes.
4. Stir in the tomato sauce and bring to a boil.
5. Reduce the heat to low and simmer for about 10 minutes.
6. Stir in the cream, paprika and 1 tbsp of the sugar and again bring to a simmer.
7. Simmer for about 10-15 minutes, stirring occasionally.
8. In another skillet, heat the vegetable oil on medium heat and sear the chicken pieces and curry powder for about 3 minutes.
9. Transfer the chicken with any pan juices into the sauce and simmer for about 30 minutes.

Inner City Curry

🥣 Prep Time: 20 mins
🕐 Total Time: 1 hr

Servings per Recipe: 4
Calories   472 kcal
Fat   40.9 g
Carbohydrates   14.6 g
Protein   27.1 g
Cholesterol   57 mg
Sodium   935 mg

Ingredients

1 lb. skinless, boneless chicken breast halves - cut into 1 inch cubes
1 tbsp dark soy sauce
1 tbsp all-purpose flour
2 tbsp cooking oil
2 tbsp green curry paste, see appendix
2 green onions with tops, chopped
3 cloves garlic, peeled and chopped
1 tsp fresh ginger, peeled and finely chopped
2 C. coconut milk
1 tbsp fish sauce
1 tbsp dark soy sauce
2 tbsp white sugar
1/2 C. cilantro leaves, for garnish

Directions

1. Coat the chicken with 1 tbsp of the dark soy sauce and then with the flour evenly.
2. In a large skillet, heat the oil on medium-high heat and cook the chicken cubes for about 5 minutes.
3. Transfer the chicken into a plate.
4. In the same skillet, sauté the curry paste on medium heat for about 1 minute.
5. Add the green onions, garlic and ginger and sauté for about 2 minutes.
6. Add the cooked chicken and stir to coat with the curry mixture.
7. Stir in the coconut milk, fish sauce, 1 tbsp of the soy sauce and sugar and simmer for about 20 minutes.
8. Serve with a garnishing of the cilantro leaves.

PINEAPPLE
Pepper Curry

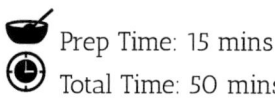

Prep Time: 15 mins
Total Time: 50 mins

Servings per Recipe: 6
Calories   623 kcal
Fat   34.5 g
Carbohydrates   77.5g
Protein   20.3 g
Cholesterol   20 mg
Sodium   781 mg

Ingredients

- 2 C. uncooked jasmine rice
- 1 quart water
- 1/4 C. red curry paste, see appendix
- 2 (13.5 oz.) cans coconut milk
- 2 skinless, boneless chicken breast halves - cut into thin strips
- 3 tbsp fish sauce
- 1/4 C. white sugar
- 1 1/2 C. sliced bamboo shoots, drained
- 1/2 red bell pepper, julienned
- 1/2 green bell pepper, julienned
- 1/2 small onion, chopped
- 1 C. pineapple chunks, drained

Directions

1. In a pan, add the rice and water and bring to a boil.
2. Reduce the heat to low and simmer, covered for about 25 minutes.
3. In a bowl, add the curry paste and 1 can of the coconut milk and beat till well combined.
4. Transfer the curry paste mixture into a wok.
5. Add the remaining coconut milk, chicken, fish sauce, sugar, and bamboo shoots and bring to a boil.
6. Cook for about 15 minutes, stirring occasionally.
7. Stir in the bell peppers and onion and cook for about 10 minutes.
8. Remove from the heat and immediately, stir in the pineapple.
9. Serve over the cooked rice.

Cape Chicken Curry

Prep Time: 20 mins
Total Time: 1 hr

Servings per Recipe: 4
Calories   600 kcal
Fat   33.4 g
Carbohydrates   13.4g
Protein   64.4 g
Cholesterol   199 mg
Sodium   452 mg

Ingredients

1 tbsp olive oil
1 onion, chopped
2 cloves garlic, peeled and chopped
1 bay leaf
1 (14.5 oz.) can whole peeled tomatoes, drained
2 tsp curry powder
1/8 tsp salt
1 (2 to 3 lb.) whole chicken, bones and skin removed, cut into pieces
1 (14 oz.) can unsweetened coconut milk
1 lemon, juiced

Directions

1. In a large, heavy skillet, heat the olive oil on medium heat and sauté the onion, garlic and bay leaf till browned lightly.
2. Stir in the tomatoes, curry powder and salt and cook for about 5 minutes.
3. Stir in the chicken and cook for about 15-20 minutes.
4. Reduce the heat to low.
5. Slowly, add the coconut milk, stirring continuously during the period of about 10 minutes.
6. Stir in the lemon juice and serve immediately.

ANJALI'S Carrot and Zucchini Curry

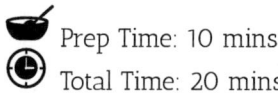

Prep Time: 10 mins
Total Time: 20 mins

Servings per Recipe: 4
Calories	271 kcal
Fat	15.8 g
Carbohydrates	11.2g
Protein	25.4 g
Cholesterol	59 mg
Sodium	147 mg

Ingredients

- 2 tsp olive oil
- 1 lb. skinless, boneless chicken breast halves - cut into thin strips
- 1 tbsp Thai red curry paste, see appendix
- 1 C. sliced halved zucchini
- 1 red bell pepper, seeded and sliced into strips
- 1/2 C. sliced carrots
- 1 onion, quartered then halved
- 1 tbsp cornstarch
- 1 (14 oz.) can light coconut milk
- 2 tbsp chopped fresh cilantro

Directions

1. In a large skillet, heat the oil on medium-high heat and cook the chicken pieces for about 3 minutes.
2. Stir in the curry paste, zucchini, bell pepper, carrot and onion and cook for a few minutes.
3. In a bowl, dissolve the cornstarch in the coconut milk.
4. Stir the cornstarch mixture in the curry and bring to a boil.
5. Reduce the heat to medium heat and simmer for about 1 minute.
6. Stir in the cilantro and serve immediately.

Backyard Tandoori

Prep Time: 10 mins
Total Time: 8 hrs 55 mins

Servings per Recipe: 8
Calories   349 kcal
Fat   20.5 g
Carbohydrates   5.4g
Protein   34.2 g
Cholesterol   120 mg
Sodium   618 mg

Ingredients

- 2 (6 oz.) containers plain yogurt
- 2 tsp kosher salt
- 1 tsp black pepper
- 1/2 tsp ground cloves
- 2 tbsp freshly grated ginger
- 3 cloves garlic, minced
- 4 tsp paprika
- 2 tsp ground cumin
- 2 tsp ground cinnamon
- 2 tsp ground coriander
- 16 chicken thighs
- olive oil spray

Directions

1. In a bowl, add the yogurt, salt, pepper, cloves, ginger, garlic, paprika, cumin, cinnamon and coriander and mix till well combined.
2. Rinse the chicken under cold water and with the paper towels, pat dry.
3. In a large resealable plastic bag, add the chicken thighs and yogurt mixture.
4. Seal the bag after squeezing out the excess air.
5. Shake the bag to coat evenly.
6. Refrigerate for about 8 hours or overnight, flipping the bag occasionally.
7. Set your outdoor grill for direct medium heat.
8. Remove the chicken from the bag and discard the marinade.
9. With the paper towels, wipe off the excess marinade.
10. Spray the chicken pieces with the olive oil spray.
11. Cook the chicken thighs on the grill for about 2 minutes per side.
12. Now, arrange the chicken thighs over the indirect heat and cook for about 35-40 minutes.

CLASSICAL
Korma

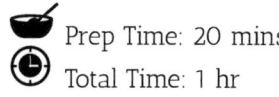

Prep Time: 20 mins
Total Time: 1 hr

Servings per Recipe: 4
Calories	398 kcal
Fat	27.5 g
Carbohydrates	13.4g
Protein	25.3 g
Cholesterol	95 mg
Sodium	477 mg

Ingredients

- 1/4 C. cashew halves
- 1/4 C. boiling water
- 3 cloves garlic, peeled
- 1 (1/2 inch) piece fresh ginger root, peeled and chopped
- 3 tbsp vegetable oil
- 2 bay leaves, crumbled
- 1 large onion, minced
- 1 tsp ground coriander
- 1 tsp garam masala
- 1 tsp ground cumin
- 1 tsp ground turmeric
- 1 tsp chili powder
- 3 skinless, boneless chicken breast halves - diced
- 1/4 C. tomato sauce
- 1 C. chicken broth
- 1/2 C. heavy cream
- 1/2 C. plain yogurt
- 1 tsp cornstarch, mixed with equal parts water

Directions

1. In a small bowl, soak the cashews in the boiling water for about 15-20 minutes.
2. In a food processor, add the garlic and ginger and pulse till smooth.
3. In a wok, heat the oil on medium heat and sauté the bay leaves for about 30 seconds.
4. Stir in the onion and cook for about 3-5 minutes.
5. Stir in the garlic paste, coriander, garam masala, cumin, turmeric and chili powder.
6. Stir in the chicken and cook for about 5 minutes.
7. Stir in the tomato sauce and chicken broth.
8. Reduce the heat and simmer, covered for about 15 minutes, stirring occasionally.
9. Meanwhile in a food processor, add the cashews with the soaking water, cream and yogurt and pulse till smooth.
10. Stir the cashew mixture in the curry and simmer for about 15 minutes, stirring occasionally.
11. Stir in the cornstarch mixture and cook for about 1-2 minutes.

Emerald Isle Curry

Prep Time: 20 mins
Total Time: 1 hr 15 mins

Servings per Recipe: 6
Calories 298 kcal
Fat 8.9 g
Carbohydrates 14.2g
Protein 38.8 g
Cholesterol 111 mg
Sodium 322 mg

Ingredients

3 tbsp butter
2 small onion, chopped
2 apples - peeled, cored and finely chopped
3 tbsp all-purpose flour
1 tbsp curry powder
8 skinless, boneless chicken breasts
1 C. hot chicken broth
1 C. milk
salt and pepper to taste

Directions

1. Set your oven to 350 degrees F before doing anything else.
2. In a pan, melt the butter on medium heat and sauté the apple till tender.
3. Add the curry powder and sauté for about 1 minute.
4. Stir in the flour and cook for about 1 minute.
5. Stir in the broth and milk and remove from the heat.
6. Season the chicken breasts with the salt and pepper evenly.
7. Arrange the chicken breasts in a 13x9-inch baking dish in a single layer.
8. Place the apple mixture over the chicken breasts evenly.
9. Cook in the oven for about 45-50 minutes.

TUESDAY'S Curry

Prep Time: 15 mins
Total Time: 1 hr 15 mins

Servings per Recipe: 4
Calories	286 kcal
Fat	9.9 g
Carbohydrates	14.9 g
Protein	31.1 g
Cholesterol	88 mg
Sodium	620 mg

Ingredients

- 4 skinless, boneless chicken breast halves
- 2 tbsp butter
- 1 onion, chopped
- 2/3 C. beer
- 1 (10.75 oz.) can condensed tomato soup
- 1 tsp curry powder
- 1/2 tsp dried basil
- 1/2 tsp ground black pepper
- 1/4 C. grated Parmesan cheese

Directions

1. Set your oven to 350 degrees F before doing anything else.
2. In a medium skillet, melt the butter on medium heat and sauté the onion till tender.
3. Stir in the beer, soup, curry powder, basil and pepper.
4. Reduce the heat to low and simmer for about 10 minutes.
5. Arrange the chicken breasts in a 13x9-inch baking dish in a single layer.
6. Place the onion mixture over the chicken breasts evenly.
7. Cook in the oven for about 50 minutes.
8. Sprinkle with the cheese and cook in the oven for about 10 minutes.

Chicken Curry 101

Prep Time: 10 mins
Total Time: 30 mins

Servings per Recipe: 6
Calories   343 kcal
Fat   24.3 g
Carbohydrates   9.8 g
Protein   22.3 g
Cholesterol   62 mg
Sodium   83 mg

Ingredients

1 (3 lb.) whole chicken, skin removed and cut into pieces
3 onions, chopped
1 tsp ground cinnamon
1 bay leaf
2 cloves crushed garlic
1/4 tsp ground ginger
1 tsp paprika
3 tbsp curry powder
1/2 tsp white sugar
1/2 lemon, juiced
1/2 tsp cayenne pepper
1 tbsp tomato paste
1 pinch salt
1/4 C. olive oil
water to cover

Directions

1. In a large skillet, heat the oil on medium heat and sauté the onion till browned.
2. Add the cinnamon, bay leaf, ginger, paprika, curry powder, sugar, salt and garlic and sauté for about 2 minutes.
3. Add the chicken pieces, tomato and enough water to just cover the chicken and simmer for about 20 minutes.
4. Stir in the lemon juice and the cayenne pepper and simmer for about 5 minutes.

CURRY
Dump Dinner

Prep Time: 20 mins
Total Time: 3 hrs 25 mins

Servings per Recipe: 4
Calories   635 kcal
Fat   37.9 g
Carbohydrates   32g
Protein   45.2 g
Cholesterol   111 mg
Sodium   2231 mg

Ingredients

1 tbsp butter
1 onion, chopped
1 (10.75 oz.) can condensed cream of mushroom soup
1 (10.75 oz.) can condensed cream of chicken soup
1 (14 oz.) can coconut milk
1 packet dry onion soup mix (such as Knorr(R) French Onion Soup Mix)
3 tbsp curry powder
1/2 tsp salt
1/2 tsp ground black pepper
2 tsp ground cayenne pepper
3 large skinless, boneless chicken breast halves -- trimmed and cut into 1-inch pieces
1 C. green peas
2 C. sliced fresh mushrooms

Directions

1. In a skillet, melt the butter on medium heat and sauté the onion for about 5-10 minutes.
2. In a large bowl, add the cream of mushroom soup, cream of chicken soup, coconut milk, dry soup mix, curry powder, salt, pepper and cayenne pepper and mix till well combined.
3. In the bottom of a slow cooker, place the chicken and top with the soup mixture and onion, peas and mushrooms and stir to combine.
4. Set the slow cooker on High.
5. Cook, covered for about 1 1/2 hours.
6. Now, set the slow cooker on Low and cook, covered for about 1 1/2-2 hours.

Simple Fruit Curry

Prep Time: 25 mins
Total Time: 35 mins

Servings per Recipe: 4
Calories   398 kcal
Fat   20.4 g
Carbohydrates   31.1g
Protein   26.5 g
Cholesterol   58 mg
Sodium   179 mg

Ingredients

- 2 medium mangoes, peeled and sliced, divided
- 1 (10 oz.) can coconut milk
- 4 tsp vegetable oil
- 4 tsp spicy curry paste, see appendix
- 14 oz. skinless, boneless chicken breast halves - cut into cubes
- 4 medium shallots, sliced
- 1 large English cucumber, seeded and sliced

Directions

1. In a blender, add half of the mango slices and coconut milk and pulse till smooth.
2. In a large pan, heat the oil on medium-high heat and sauté the curry paste for about 1 minute.
3. Add the chicken and shallot and cook for about 5 minutes.
4. Stir in the mango puree and cook till heated completely.
5. Stir in the remaining mango slices and cucumber and serve immediately.

Manufactured by Amazon.ca
Bolton, ON

27270674R00039